W9-AOE-905

Date: 8/30/19

J 307.76 KIN
King, Madeline,
Cities /

World Book, Inc.
180 North LaSalle Street
Suite 900
Chicago, Illinois 60601
USA

For information about other "True or False?" titles, as
well as other World Book print and digital publications,
please go to www.worldbook.com.

For information about other World Book publications,
call 1-800-WORLDBK (967-5325).

For information about sales to schools and libraries,
call 1-800-975-3250 (United States) or 1-800-837-5365
(Canada).

Library of Congress Cataloging-in-Publication Data for
this volume has been applied for.

True or False?
ISBN: 978-0-7166-3761-5 (set, hc.)

Cities
ISBN: 978-0-7166-3763-9 (hc.)

Also available as:
ISBN: 978-0-7166-3773-8 (e-book, ePUB3)

Printed in China by RR Donnelley,
Guangdong Province
1st printing May 2019

Staff

CITIES

WORLD
BOOK

www.worldbook.com

TRUE OR FALSE?

Cities cover 15 percent of
Earth's surface.

Cities cover less than
1 percent of Earth's
surface.

More than half of the world's population lives in cities.

Around 55 percent of the world's population now lives in a city or an urban area, according to the United Nations.

In Bogotá *(BOH guh TAH)*, Colombia, a country in South America, *mimes* (actors who don't use words) used to make fun of drivers who broke traffic laws.

City officials in Bogotá once hired "traffic mimes" and human "cones" to embarrass drivers doing the wrong thing and to cheer those doing the right thing—silently or boisterously, of course!

TRUE OR FALSE?

Brasília *(brah SEEL yuh)*, the capital of Brazil, was designed to look like a bicycle.

17

FALSE!

When seen from the air, Brasília resembles the shape of a drawn bow and arrow.

In Singapore, it is against the law to chew gum.

And the list of unlawful things does not stop there. Some unlawful acts include selling gum, annoying someone with a musical instrument, flying a kite that harms public traffic, and forgetting to flush the toilet!

TRUE OR FALSE?

Residents of Reykjavik *(RAY kyuh VEEK)*, Iceland, cannot own dogs.

Keeping pooches as pets is no longer against the law in Reykjavik. But for 60 years, dogs were banned—between 1924 and 1984. It was thought that dogs were farm animals and not suited for city living. Also, it was discovered that dogs carried a parasite that could be harmful to people. For residents and man's best friend, the ban must have been *ruff!*

The famous "Hollywood" sign in Los Angeles, California, used to read "Movieland."

In very big letters, the sign used to spell "Hollywoodland." Today's widely recognized "Hollywood" sign was rebuilt in the late 1970's.

30

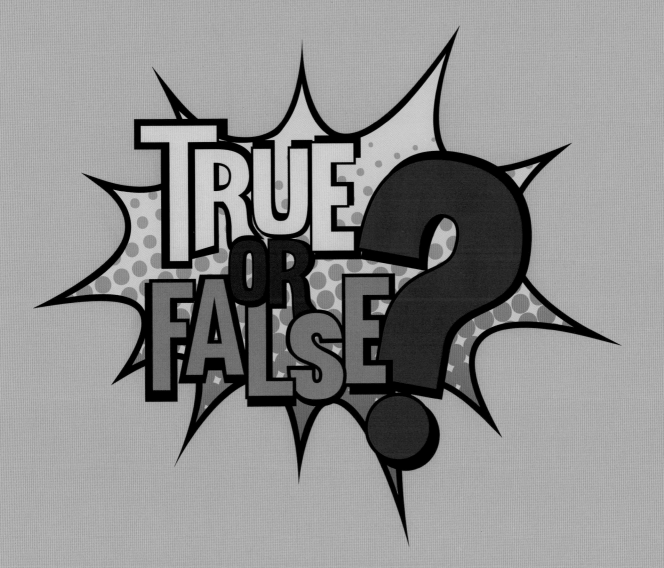

Cairo *(KY roh)*, Egypt, is nicknamed
the *City of Light*.

Cairo is nicknamed the *City of a Thousand Minarets*. A *minaret* is a tall, slender tower that is part of a *mosque,* or a place where Muslims worship. Paris, France, is nicknamed the *City of Light*.

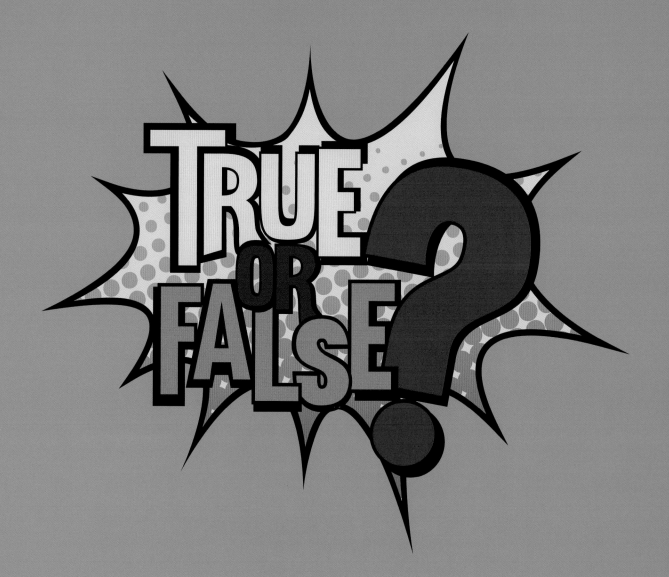

Barcelona, Spain, has a
chocolate museum.

The Museu de la Xocolata *(moo ZAY oh day lah choh koh LAH tah)* has chocolate sculptures of famous buildings in Barcelona! The ticket to enter the museum is a free chocolate bar with the flag of the visitor's home country on it. *Yum!*

Cape Town, South Africa, is known as the *Tavern of the Seas.*

Cape Town lies close to the meeting point of the Atlantic and Indian oceans. Jan van Riebeeck, an employee of the Dutch East India Company, arrived there in April 1652 to set up a refreshment station for company sailors. Cape Town is still known as the *Tavern of the Seas* today.

TRUE OR FALSE?

It takes more than 100 letters to write the full Thai name of Bangkok *(BANG kok)*, Thailand, in the English alphabet.

44

Krung Thep Mahanakhon Amon Rattanakosin Mahinthara Ayuthaya Mahadilok Phop Noppharat wathani Burirom Udomratchaniwet Mahasathan Amon Piman Awatan Sathit Sakkathattiya Witsanukam Prasit

TRUE!

The full name of Bangkok uses 168 letters: Krung Thep Mahanakhon Amon Rattanakosin Mahinthara Ayuthaya Mahadilok Phop Noppharat Ratchathani Burirom Udomratchaniwet Mahasathan Amon Piman Awatan Sathit Sakkathattiya Witsanukam Prasit.

New York City, in the U.S. state of New York, has the longest train system in the world.

Shanghai *(SHANG hy)*, China, has the longest train system in the world. It is 365 miles (588 kilometers) long!

107

TRUE OR FALSE?

Copenhagen, Denmark, is designed in the shape of a hand.

53

Copenhagen uses the "(Five) Finger Plan." The city center is the "palm" and the living areas are the "fingers."

TRUE OR FALSE?

The U.S. city of Anchorage, Alaska, is the coldest city in the world.

Yakutsk, Russia, is the coldest city in the world. The coldest temperature on record in this Siberian city was about -84 °F (-64 °C) in 1891. *Brrr!*

59

TRUE OR FALSE?

Tokyo, Japan, has more people than any other city in the world.

60

The population of Tokyo is over 38 million people. Delhi *(DEHL ee)*, India, is second with almost 28 million people.

Irkutsk, in Siberia, Russia, is famous for having the shallowest lake in the world, with a record depth of 4 inches (10 centimeters).

Irkutsk is noted for nearby Lake Baikal *(by KAHL)*—the oldest and deepest lake in the world. Lake Baikal is 5,315 feet (1,620 meters) deep. It formed about 25 million years ago.

TRUE OR FALSE?

In Montreal (*MON tree AWL*), Canada, people can travel almost anywhere underground.

TRUE!

There is a group of connecting tunnels underneath Montreal. In the winter, the more than 20 miles (32 kilometers) of tunnels make it easy for people to go to such places as shopping malls, museums, restaurants, and offices.

Niveau Galerie

Niveau Ste-Catherine

Niveau Métro
↓ Niveau Tunnel ↓

ESPACE RESTOS

L'AVENIR S'ANNONCE chic

71

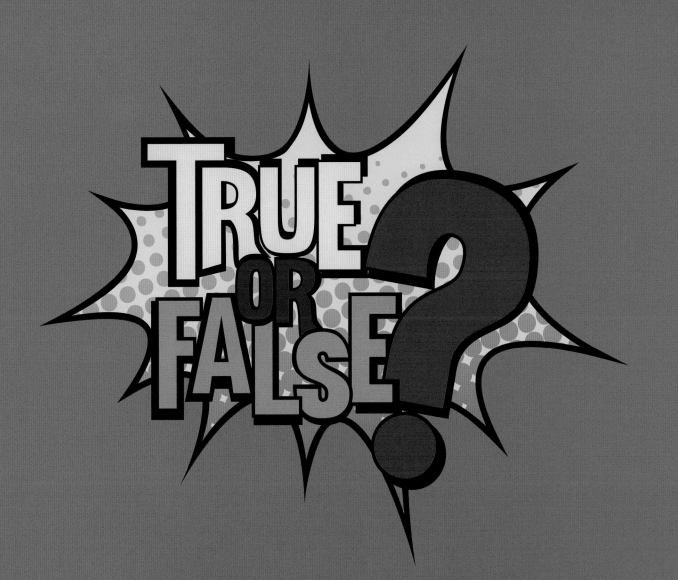

The world's largest palace is in the
city of Agra *(AH gruh)*, India.

FALSE!

Beijing *(bay jihng)*, China, has the world's largest palace, the Forbidden City.

TRUE OR FALSE?

Peru *(puh ROO)* is home to a place called the *Lost City.*

TRUE!

The name of the place is Machu Picchu *(MAH choo PEEK choo* or *MAH choo PEE choo)*. It was a city built by the Inca civilization. Machu Picchu probably housed members of the Inca royal family. It is located high on a ridge in the Andes Mountains.

TRUE OR FALSE?

The U.S. city of Chicago, Illinois, had the first Ferris wheel.

The first Ferris wheel was **264 feet (80.5 meters)** tall. It made its first appearance at the **1893 World's Columbian Exposition** in **Chicago**. Today, a **196-foot- (59.7-meter-) tall Centennial Wheel** graces the city's skyline.

TRUE OR FALSE?

Rome, Italy, has a fountain where visitors throw $1 billion worth of coins into the water each year.

However, visitors to Trevi *(TREH vee)* Fountain in Rome do throw about $800,000 worth of coins into that fountain, and all of the money goes to charity.

TRUE OR FALSE?

Mexico City, Mexico, rises 2 inches (5 centimeters) higher each year.

Sadly, Mexico City sinks 3.2 feet (1 meter) each year. In the last few decades, the city has sunk more than 30 feet (9 meters). That's because the people are using up the groundwater that comes from under the city.

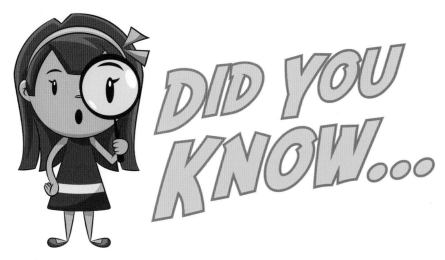

DID YOU KNOW...

In Mumbai *(mum BY)*, India, there is a lunchbox delivery service. *Dabbawalas*, or *ones who carry the box*, deliver the food. Every day **for over 100 years,** dabbawalas have delivered hot, homecooked meals to people all over the city.

The U.S. city of Boston, Massachusetts, was once submerged in molasses! It was the "Great Molasses Flood." In 1919, a giant steel holding tank with 2.3 million gallons (9 million liters) of molasses exploded, sending a wall of the sticky syrup rushing through Boston streets.

October 31st is
World Cities Day.
The first celebration was held in Shanghai, China, in 2014.

In 1924, the city of San Francisco, California, **dug up most of its dead** and reburied them in the little town of Colma, California. Now Colma, known as the *City of Souls*, has more dead people (1.5 million) than living people (1,509).

A lot of people are already making plans for **cities in space.** Some plans are so imaginative they are nearly out of this world! One plan calls for a city on Mars with a million people in 50 years.

Index

Acknowledgments

Cover: © Djomas/Shutterstock; © Diego Schtutman, Shutterstock

5-10 © Shutterstock

13 © Krzysztof Dydynski, Getty Images

14 © Ariana Cubillos, AP/Shutterstock

16 © Evaristo Sa, AFP/Getty Images

19 © 061 Filmes/Shutterstock

20 © Pete Ark, Getty Images

23 © Silent Wings/Shutterstock

24-27 © Bjarki Reyr, Getty Images

29 ©Tono Balaguer, Shutterstock

31 © Underwood Archives/Getty Images

32-37 © Shutterstock

39 © Steve Vidler, Alamy Images

40 © Guilherme Mesquita, Shutterstock

43 © Nastasic/Getty Images

45-57 © Shutterstock

59 © Amos Chapple, Getty Images

61 © Lewis Tse Pui Lung, Shutterstock

62 © Gerhard Joren, Getty Images

65-75 © Shutterstock

77-79 ©WIN-Initiative/Getty Images

80-81 © Luis Enrique Torres, Shutterstock

82 Public Domain

84-90 © Shutterstock

92 © Shutterstock; © Bettmann/Getty Images

93-96 Shutterstock